After its launch w　　　　　 ..gain and again, and the US President, Donald Trump, failed to obtain a court order preventing its publication, the memoirs of the former National Security Adviser, John Bolton, were finally issued in his new book entitled: "The Room That Saw the Events."

Bolton's new book was due to be officially launched on Tuesday 23 June, although a pirated electronic version appeared 48 hours earlier.

Bolton recounts his story with Trump and the various stages he went through from Trump's victory in the presidency, until his appointment as National Security Adviser, all the way to his resignation in September last year. Bolton's new book relays the picture from inside the White House, just as none of those who entered the Trump administration did it, and it tells about many issues in which Trump had controversial positions, explaining their backgrounds and what went on between his ministers and advisors behind the scenes, and among these issues: the American withdrawal from Syria and Iraq, and the assassination of the journalist Saudi Khashoggi, how to deal with Russia, the political and economic relationship with China, the withdrawal from

NATO, and the peace agreement with the Taliban.

In the following lines, we provide a comprehensive overview of the main themes included in Bolton's new book, published by Simon & Schuster Publishing.

SECOND READING IN JOHN BOLTON*S / THE ROOM WHERE IT HAPPENED   a White House Memoir

SECOND READING BY ILYASS BOURICH

After postponing its launch again and again, and the failure of the US President, Donald Trump, to obtain a court order preventing its publication, the memoirs of the former National Security Adviser, John Bolton, were finally issued in his new book entitled: "The Room That Witnessed the Events", in 570 pages, divided into 15 chapters, in addition to a photo album showing the most prominent personalities the author met, and the most important stations he witnessed.

Bolton's new book was due to be officially launched yesterday, Tuesday, June 23, although a pirated electronic version appeared 48 hours earlier.

Bolton recounts his story with Trump and the various stages he went through from Trump's victory in the presidency, until his appointment as National Security Adviser, all the way to his resignation in September last year. Bolton's new book relays the picture from inside the White House, just as none of those who entered the Trump administration did it, and it tells about many issues in which Trump had controversial positions, explaining their backgrounds and what went on between his ministers and advisors behind the scenes, and among these issues: the American withdrawal from Syria and Iraq, and the assassination of the journalist Saudi Khashoggi, how to deal with Russia, the political and economic relationship with China, the withdrawal from NATO, and the peace agreement with the Taliban.

In the following lines, we provide a comprehensive overview of the main themes included in Bolton's new book, published by Simon and Schuster Publishing.

1. The Long Walk to the West Wing Office

In the first chapter of the book, Bolton reviews the circumstances in which he assumed the position of National Security Adviser in the Trump administration, saying: When you work as a national security advisor, you are attracted by the many challenges that you face. If you are averse to unrest, and don't like meeting international and local personalities, try something else. Working in such a location is exhilarating, but difficult to fathom.

The "Al-Rashideen Axis" ... Has it succeeded in restraining Trump?

In his book, Bolton is unable to provide a comprehensive theory of the Trump administration's transformation. Because, in his opinion, that is not possible. And the truth he concluded is that Trump has always been a stranger and hesitant; For the first 15 months, he succumbed to the "Al-Rashideen Axis" (a term used in Washington to refer to: generals, business leaders, and Republican Party members who struggle to steer the president's helm and curb his subversive whims). However, with the passage of time, he became more confident, surrounded by only bright women - as Bolton described - and the "axis of adults" caused permanent problems. Not because they managed the Trump administration successfully, but because they failed to do so.

Bolton adds: I have long believed that the task of the National Security Adviser is to make sure that the president understands the options available to him to make the right decision, and then to make sure that the stakeholders implement that decision.

But the "axis of adults" served Trump very badly, by pursuing their personal interest and publicly condemning Trump's goals, which raised Trump's suspicions of those around him. However, the author added: The "adult axis" is not entirely responsible for this mentality, as Trump is Trump.

Bolton's desire for the position of National Security Adviser

The author adds: After less than a month in the administration, Mike Flynn, the National Security Adviser, self-sabotaged and lost Trump's complete confidence. Unfortunately, confusion and disruption were the hallmarks of NSC employees in the first three weeks of the administration. The press speculated that Flynn's successor would be another general.

On Friday, February 17th (Shabat), Steve Bannon texted Bolton asking him to come to Mar Alago to meet Trump over the weekend. When Bolton arrived, one of the guests told him that he had heard Trump say several times: 'I am really starting to love Bolton.'

Trump greeted him warmly, expressing his respect and happiness with his nomination as a national security advisor, and offered him other positions, so Bolton politely refused, saying, "I'm only interested in the job of National Security Adviser." On his way to Washington, DC, while on the plane, Bolton learned that Trump had chosen Herbert McMaster as his national security advisor.

Bolton's first advice to Trump

Bolton returned to the White House in June to see Trump, congratulating him on pulling out of the Paris climate agreement, and warning him against wasting political capital to achieve the elusive goal of resolving the Arab-Israeli conflict.

Bolton strongly supported moving the US

embassy in Israel to Jerusalem, and recognizing it as the capital of Israel. Regarding Iran, Trump urged to proceed with withdrawing from the nuclear agreement, but while Bolton was warning against the use of violence in this file and nominating him as the last option, Trump on the other hand was expressing his support for Netanyahu if he made a decision to violence against Iran.

Around this time, a Russian assassination squad attacked former Russian spy Sergey Skripal and his daughter in the English city of Salisbury. Prime Minister Theresa May expelled twenty-three secret Russian intelligence agents.

Despite his call with Putin, in which he congratulated him on his re-election, Trump later expelled more than 60 Russian "diplomats" to show solidarity with London. On Wednesday, March 21, 2018, Bolton received a call from Trump in which he said, "I have a job for you that may be the strongest job in the White House." And when he began to answer, Trump added: "No, really better than the Chief of Staff." The call ended with an agreement to meet Trump in the Oval Office the next day. And they talked about Iran and North Korea.

Later, Trump tweeted, "I am pleased to announce that, starting 9/4/2018, John Bolton will be the new National Security Adviser."

What motivated Bolton to accept this job?

"Because America faced a very dangerous international environment, and I thought I knew what to do," Bolton replies. I had strong views on a wide range of issues. "

What about Trump? "No one can claim at this point that they do not know the size of the risks involved, but I also thought that I could deal with them," Bolton replies.

I have watched Trump closely during the nearly

15 months in office, had no illusions that I could change him, and I resolved to conduct a disciplined and comprehensive process, but I will judge my performance by how the policy is actually shaped, not by comparison with my performance with Previous administrations.

2. Cry over ruin .. and release the dogs of war!

The second chapter of Bolton's new book began by restoring the scene of the Syrian army's use of chemical weapons in the attack on the city of Douma and other areas close to it, which resulted in dozens of dead and hundreds of wounded, so the United States of America responded firmly by launching 59 cruise missiles at Suspicious sites.

The Syrian dictatorship has not learned the lesson, and American deterrence has failed, and the concern is how to respond properly, according to Bolton in his book, pointing to President Trump's tweet, in which he condemned the killing of innocent people as a result of the chemical attack that isolated the region from the whole world, considering Putin and Russia And Iran is responsible for these atrocities for supporting the "animal" lion.

The biggest danger in Bolton's view: Iran

The author notes that the suggestion of Jack Keane, a former deputy chief of staff in the US Army, was applauded by Trump when he saw it on Fox News. Kane proposed destroying the five main war airfields in Syria, which would result in the defeat of Assad's forces. On that day, France and Britain showed their support for the US-led military offensive.

However, what is happening in Syria, whoever rules it, would not have distracted the United States from the real danger - in Bolton's view - which is Iran.

The real obstacle, according to Matisse: Russia

On the other hand, US Defense Secretary Jim

Mattis saw Russia as the real obstacle, and he attributed this to Obama's unwise agreement with Putin in 2014 regarding ending Syria's ability in the field of chemical weapons, which clearly did not happen.

Bolton warns in his book that the Trump administration has not made a final decision on the American withdrawal from Syria, but it has considered it necessary to curb Iran in the event of an American withdrawal, which he discussed with his British counterpart, Mark Sedwell, in his first calls with an external official, and he was surprised At the time, Sedwell with an intention to withdraw, which he had not known about before.

Bolton describes how Macron phoned Trump, urged him to take immediate action, and threatened that France would act alone in the event of a delay by the United States. Although his threat was showcasing in Bolton's view, Macron was right to take immediate and decisive action, because the faster the retribution was, the clearer the message became to Assad and others.

Erdogan is avoiding getting involved in the American attack ... and "lecturing" Trump and Bolton

While briefing Trump on developments before his phone call with Turkish President Recep Tayyip Erdogan, Bolton assured him that they had come up with the appropriate formula:

First: a triple attack (the United States - France - Britain), not a unilateral attack by the United States only. Second: Adopting a comprehensive approach using all political and economic as well as military means, accompanied by an explanation regarding this procedure and its reason. Third: Make a sustainable effort. Trump seemed convinced of this formula.

Bolton indicated his annoyance with Erdoan in the call later that day, likening his strength and tone in the call to Mussolini's speech from the balcony in front of audiences, and seemed to be giving a lecture to them. Erdogan has evaded any commitment to join the US attack plots and has said he will speak to Putin sooner, according to Bolton. The next day, Bolton received a call from his Turkish counterpart, Ibrahim Kalin, to inform him about what happened between Erdogan and Putin, and that the latter confirmed his desire not to get involved in a confrontation with the United States over Syria, and that everyone should act rationally.

Have we succeeded in deterring the lion?

The United States launched an attack on April 7, 2017, which was limited to Syrian facilities that contained chemical weapons, including headquarters, aircraft and all related targets, but did not pose a fundamental threat to the Syrian regime itself, which made Assad, Russia and Iran breathe a sigh of relief. .

About a year after that attack, Trump agreed to

launch an attack on the Assad regime, in coordination with France and Britain this time, and the Syrian defenses were unable to intercept American cruise missiles.

At the end of the chapter, the author wonders: Have we succeeded in deterring Assad? He replied, "No, we did not, because Assad began using chemical weapons again against civilians in May 2019."

3. America Free

The third chapter of Bolton's book reviewed, at its beginning, the facts of Trump's meeting with the Japanese President, Shinzo Abe, which focused on political and security issues, such as the issue of North Korea, as well as economic affairs and trade, noting that Trump praised Japan as the best ally of the United States. At the same time, he criticized its attack on Pearl Harbor during World War II (1941).

The next day, Trump and Abe held a press

conference, and Bolton counted the summit as a real success on technical issues, such as North Korea.

Behind the scenes of withdrawal from the nuclear deal with Iran

Bolton moved to talk about withdrawing from the Iranian nuclear deal, explaining that he had always believed that Iran's possession of nuclear weapons was a threat, because it might encourage countries in the Middle East, such as Turkey, Egypt and Saudi Arabia, to acquire their nuclear weapons, as well as Iran's sponsorship of terrorism in the Middle East, And providing weapons to terrorist groups loyal to it.

"The European Union is worse than China, but the difference is that it is smaller than China."

Trump

Bolton reviewed some of the scenes of the period before Trump announced the withdrawal from the Iranian agreement, specifically when the US President informed his French counterpart of his intention to withdraw from the agreement, Macron replied, saying: "Nobody thinks that it is enough" and argued that "a new comprehensive agreement must be worked out." This is the view supported by the British Foreign Secretary at the time, Boris Johnson.

The author moved to Trump's meeting with Merkel, in which the German chancellor asked the Americans not to withdraw from the agreement, but talking about it was not organized, and Trump's reaction was indifferent. At the same meeting, Trump repeated a sentence that Bolton says he heard countless later: "The European Union is worse than China, it is only smaller than it."

4. Kim and Trump in Singapore

The fourth chapter of Bolton's new book begins with the approaching US withdrawal from the

Iran nuclear deal, when Trump resumed his focus on the North Korean nuclear project, and arrangements began to hold his meeting with Kim, a meeting that Trump was interested in since the beginning of his rule, according to what Pompeo told Bolton, who He was pessimistic at the time because North Korea had previously lured the United States and other countries to the negotiating table, in exchange for economic benefits and time, despite its obligations being repeatedly violated.

Bolton says it was South Korea's national security adviser who introduced Kim's invitation to meet Trump, but then admitted that he was the one who suggested Kim that he invite Trump to a meeting with him. Bolton explains that the entire diplomatic adventure was related to South Korea's aspirations for unity with the North, and not to the constants of US policy toward Kim.

Bolton hopes Trump's meeting with Kim will collapse

The Japanese believed that North Korea should start dismantling the nuclear program immediately, provided that it should not take more than two years from Trump's agreement with Kim, but Bolton believed that this should not exceed six months, based on the experience of Libya. And when Japan indicated that North Korea had kidnapped Japanese citizens over the years, Trump pledged to pursue the case with Kim Jong Un.

Bolton recounts in his book that Kim wanted to hold his meeting with Trump in Pyongyang, or Boomingom on the border between North and South Korea, which Bolton and Pompeo agreed was unacceptable.

Pompeo thought Geneva or Singapore were the best acceptable places, but Kim does not like flying. Also, none of North Korea's ramshackle planes can reach any city, and he doesn't want to be far from Pyongyang. Bolton had hoped that all of this would lead to the collapse of the entire meeting.

A "propaganda hoax" ... North Korea announces to stop nuclear and ballistic tests

North Korea announced that it would abandon any other nuclear or ballistic tests because it was already a nuclear power. The media described this as a good step, and Trump said it was a "great progress", while Bolton viewed it only as a "propaganda trick," as he mentions in his book.

South Korean President Moon Jae-in asked Kim to denuclearize within a year, and Kim agreed, but in the months that followed, convincing the Foreign Ministry to agree to a one-year timetable was more difficult than convincing Kim.

Moon met Trump and praised the leadership role of the US president, who urged him to tell South Korean media how he (Trump) was responsible for all of this, Bolton says in his book.

Trump asks Bolton to praise him more on television

Japan, unlike South Korea, did not trust Kim and wanted concrete, clear and unequivocal commitments on the nuclear issue and the issue of the kidnappers. The Japanese prime minister assured Trump that he is stronger than Obama, which shows that Abe thought it necessary to remind Trump of this point.

Bolton recounts that Trump called him in about his appearances on two talk shows, during which much of the discussion focused on North Korea. Trump told him that he "did very well on television," but he should pay tribute to Trump more, "because no such thing happened before," and he meant his meeting with Kim.

Trump did not understand the Arab Spring

Bolton says Trump failed to understand the Arab Spring, which no one expected when it swept through the region in 2011, and that it was the cause of Gaddafi's downfall, not Gaddafi's abandonment of nuclear weapons in 2003.

Bolton explains that North Korea continued to threaten to cancel the meeting between Trump and Kim, and attacked Bolton by name. North Korean officials said they only felt disgust for him.

Trump manages his foreign relations similar to his female relationships

By May 21, the North Korean team had not arrived in Singapore. Trump began to wonder what happened. "I want to get out of Singapore before they leave," he told Bolton. He explained to Bolton how, with the women he'd been dating, he never liked that the breakup came from them, but rather from him.

Mike Pence and Bolton discussed the possibility of canceling the meeting, and Trump said he would tweet after dinner. But when they woke up the next day, there were no Trump tweets. Trump later said his phone was not working that night, and indicated that he wanted to know what the South Korean president thought before canceling.

Trump wanted to meet with North Korea at any cost

However, the North Korean Deputy Foreign Minister launched a scathing attack on Pence, describing him as a "political puppet" and threatening to launch a nuclear war because of Pence's comments in an interview on "Fox News".

Bolton says he advised US officials to ask North Korea to apologize or threaten to cancel the

Singapore meeting. Unless Pyongyang offered an apology.

Trump turned a blind eye to the matter at first, then asked for the full text of the North Korean deputy foreign minister's criticisms, and when he read it, he said: "This is a strong word."

Less than 12 hours after canceling the Singapore meeting, Trump used the less-offensive statement of another North Korean official at the State Department to put the June 12 meeting back on the schedule. This was a public admission that Trump wanted to meet at any cost, according to Bolton.

The dispute over the phrase "nuclear disarmament"

In the talks in the demilitarized zone between the two Koreas, the North Koreans refused to use the word "denuclearization" in the agenda of Kim and Trump's talks, the Foreign Ministry began to back down, and so did Trump, who was looking for "success" in Singapore.

Trump agreed to drop the phrase "denuclearization" from the statement. Then Kim Jong-chul, the North Korean leader's brother, was summoned to meet him at the White House, and he was carrying a letter from his brother, the Korean president, to Trump.

Trump: "It will take longer than I initially thought."

"The speech is very friendly, don't you think so?" Said Trump, who agreed to curtail military exercises for South Korea and the United States, after the meeting. Bolton agreed, but added that it was devoid of content. "We'll have a meeting to get to know each other, and then see what happens," Trump said. It will take longer than I initially thought, "he said.

After Trump got off the plane in Singapore, he

decided he didn't want to wait until Tuesday to meet Kim, and wanted to meet him on Monday. US officials had arranged for Trump to rest from the hassle of traveling before he met Kim face to face, but the less time he stayed in Singapore, the less US concessions, according to Bolton.

Kim asked Trump how to rate him? Trump said he liked the question, and that he viewed Kim as being intelligent, very kind, completely loyal, and had a great personality.

Bolton recounts that during Kim's meeting with Trump, the US president said he knew he and Kim would do well together. In response, Kim asked Trump, how do you rate him? Trump said he liked the question, and that he viewed Kim as being intelligent, a very good person, completely loyal, and had a great personality. Bolton agrees with Trump that the point of that question was to elicit a positive response from Trump.

Promised prosperity if North Korea gives up its nuclear weapons

As the meeting went on, Kim congratulated himself and Trump for what he had accomplished within an hour, and Trump agreed that others would not have been able to do so. And the two laughed. The Americans presented to the Koreans a movie prepared by the US State Department about the prosperity that North Korea could live in if it gave up its nuclear weapons, and the Koreans started watching the Korean version of the movie on an iPad.

When the film ended, Trump and Kim wanted to sign the joint statement as soon as possible, but it turned out that the inaccuracy of the translation was a hindrance; So the talks continued, and shortly after, the official photographers entered the two teams and the meeting ended.

5. A Tale of Three Cities: Brussels, London and

Helsinki

In Chapter Five, Bolton talks about three successive summits that were held in July 2018, a month after Trump and Kim Jong Un met in Singapore: the NATO meeting in Brussels with partners in the most important American alliance, and Trump's meeting with the prime minister. The British then, Theresa May, and finally Trump and Putin meeting in the Finnish capital, Helsinki, which is a neutral territory for Russia to meet.

Before leaving Washington, Trump said: "... honestly, the Putin meeting may be the easiest of them." Bolton explained that he realized during that busy July that Trump did not follow any major international strategy, or even any fixed path, and that his thinking was like an archipelago of points, leaving the rest of the aides to formulate policy, something that had its pros and cons.

"I tell the Russians that we will do whatever they want."

Bolton explained how Helsinki was chosen to hold the summit. Trump wanted Putin to visit Washington, which the Russians did not want. Washington suggested Helsinki, and Moscow suggested Vienna. It turned out that Trump was not in favor of Helsinki. John Kelly asked whether Finland was part of Russia, and when Bolton tried to explain the history of this region, Trump told him that he wanted Vienna too, and added: "I tell the Russians that we will do whatever they want." However, he settled on Helsinki after his advisors convinced him.

During preparations for the Helsinki meeting, Bolton continued to press the issue of election interference, but Russian Foreign Minister Sergey Lavrov tried to avoid it by saying that although they could not rule out the presence of hackers, the Russian government had nothing to do with it.

Putin: We do not need Iran in Syria

During Bolton's meeting with the Russian President, Putin said that the Russians do not need Iran in Syria, and that Tehran has its own agenda - related to Lebanon and the Shiites - which has nothing to do with Russian goals, but rather creates problems for them and Assad, and he made clear that Russia's goal is to support the Syrian state to prevent Chaos, as in Afghanistan, while Iran has broader goals.

Putin also indicated that the withdrawal of the Iranians means that the Syrian regime forces will lose those who protect them from the attacks of the opposition and their Western backers, and Bolton confirms that Russia is not ready to fill this vacuum.

Putin also mocked America's withdrawal from the nuclear agreement - as stated in the book - wondering what would happen if Iran withdrew, especially since Israel could not launch military action against it alone. Because it does not have the resources or capabilities, especially if the Arabs united behind Iran, which Bolton considered absurd.

At the end of the meeting, Bolton came to the view that Putin is completely in control of his nerves, confident of himself, and fully aware of Russian national security priorities, and therefore should not be left alone in a room with Trump.

Embed from Getty Images

Despite its shortcomings, NATO is the most successful political and military alliance in history

Bolton expressed his belief that despite NATO's shortcomings, it remains the most successful political and military alliance in history, and that it is primarily in the interest of Washington, not because it leases its army to defend Europe. Rather, it is because defending "the West" has always been in America's strategic interest.

During Trump's first NATO summit in 2017, the US president complained that many members had not fulfilled their 2014 commitment to spend 2% of GDP on defense by 2024, except that he focused on criticizing Germany specifically - perhaps because of his father's German origin. It spent about 1.2% of its output only on defense. Trump had asked Macron, in the consultations prior to the joint military strike in Syria, why Germany was absent from the attack, and it was a valid question, but there was no answer to it except for "domestic policy in Germany," according to Bolton.

Trump indicated that his country paid between 80-90% of NATO's expenditures, then returned later and said that it had paid 100% of the alliance's expenses, a figure unknown to the source, and threatened that America would not pay more than Germany.

Bolton's advice: Pressure on NATO members without threatening to withdraw

Bolton refers to the circumstances of this crisis with the alliance, saying that he agreed with Pompeo to persuade Trump without directly exposure to the NATO file, by saying that the Republicans cannot be charged with new controversial issues, especially with the presence of many internal battles underway (including the appointment of Judge Kavanaugh In the Supreme Court).

During their meeting with Trump on July 2, they explained to him why they had not fought more battles than they could handle, and were surprised by Trump's approval without question. Nevertheless, he returned and asked Bolton a few days later: Why does Washington not withdraw from NATO altogether? Which is exactly what they were trying to prevent. Then, in the following days, he began tweeting about this, including many of the numbers he mentioned earlier.

Bolton stated that Trump's general approach - as he explicitly stated in a call between them in Brussels - is that: By January 1, 2019, all countries must commit to 2%, otherwise America will exit the alliance and will not defend those who do not pay.

During the session, Bolton urged him to criticize belated members for not spending enough on defense, but without threatening to withdraw from the alliance or cut off American funding. Trump nodded and said nothing. Bolton explained that one of the reasons for his stay at work was Trump's commitment to do so, during his speech, and his indication that he was a supporter of NATO, and that his remarks should not be interpreted as an explicit threat to leave.

Netanyahu's demand: the establishment of "permanent borders" on the Golan Heights

Bolton said that Trump and his entourage then flew to London, where they attended a military parade before the formal meeting with their British counterparts. He explained that the dialogue initially revolved around Yemen, then moved to Syria, how to deal with the Russian presence there, and what Putin said to Bolton weeks ago regarding work to get Iran out of Syria, but May questioned Putin's words and denounced Bolton for believing him. Then the discussion moved about the issue of the attempt to assassinate the Russian dissident Sergei Skripal and his daughter, and Moscow's motives for its implementation.

He added that they then headed to the Trump resort in Turnberry, Scotland, where Trump made several calls with Israeli Prime Minister Benjamin Netanyahu, about the latter's meeting with Putin, who told him that Iran should leave Syria, but Assad has problems that prevent Putin from pushing him to pressure the Iranians. Especially his reliance on Iranian forces to make progress in Idlib against the opposition and terrorist groups. Netanyahu pressed Putin to establish a "permanent border" on the Golan Heights, but Bolton was skeptical that Trump would raise this particular issue with Putin.

Why does Trump refuse to acknowledge Russian interference in the elections?

During the first discussion between Bolton and Trump after leaving London and arriving in the Finnish capital Helsinki, Bolton made it clear that Trump remained, as he had been from the start, unwilling - or unable to recognize - any Russian interference in the US elections; Because he feared that this would undermine the legitimacy of his election and continue the "witch hunt" against him.

After a quick meeting with the Finnish President, Sauli Niinistö, who warned Trump that he must respond to Putin if he attacked him - because Putin was a fighter - news arrived that Putin's plane left Moscow late, as Putin's habit of making his guests wait.

Bolton said he was hoping this would anger

Trump; To be even tougher with Putin. Adding that they considered canceling the meeting if Putin was too late, and they decided to make him wait for a while in the Finnish Presidential Palace, where the summit will take place.

The meeting lasted about two hours, Putin spoke for the vast majority of them, and most of the talk was about Syria. Bolton considered that the final result of the summit is: no agreement on anything. But despite the lack of successes, no concessions were made, and there was no real change in foreign policy, which made him happy because he saw that his goal at this summit was: control of damage.

Putin and Trump's Priority: Increasing Trade and Investment in Russia

During the dinner that followed the summit, a superficial speech touched upon the issue of arms control, and the borders between Syria and Israel that he mentioned to Netanyahu. What they both really wanted to discuss was increasing US trade and investment in Russia, a conversation that has been going on for a long time.

Bolton added in his book that Putin emphasized during the press conference that followed that the Russian state had never interfered and would not interfere in American internal affairs, including the election process, but he said that he wanted Trump to win the 2016 elections "because he talked about restoring US relations. Russian back to normal. ' Trump confirmed that, for his part, saying: He did not see a reason for this, and that despite his confidence in intelligence, Putin's denial was clear.

He explained that Trump - who was amazed at the negative reaction in Washington to his statements - admitted in a meeting at the White House, the next day, that he had made a mistake in the sentence "I do not see any reason why (the country that interfered in the elections) should be Russia." As he intended "… it was not [Russia] that intervened," and thus the meaning of the sentence reversed. Bolton considered this was surprising, because Trump is not holding back anything he says.

6. Thwarting Russia's Attempts: Destroying the INF Treaty

In Chapter Six of Bolton's book, a former Trump advisor spoke of his desire, since the administration of President George W. Bush, to get rid of the Intermediate-Range Nuclear Forces (INF) treaty between the United States of America and the Soviet Union, which aims to eliminate medium and short-range missiles.

He points out that Russia has been violating the treaty for years, while the United States has been abiding by its provisions; What disturbed the global strategic reality and technological progress. Before Trump took office, Russia began the actual deployment of the missiles; In violation of the treaty, it posed a major threat to European NATO members.

To adjust cooperation between the US and

Russian national security agencies, Bolton suggested to the Secretary of the Russian Security Council, Nikolai Patrushev, to meet in Geneva to discuss Russian violations of the treaty. Bolton then went to Kiev to participate in the Ukrainian Independence Day celebrations, and to consult President Petro Poroshenko, his prime minister, and other officials, and briefed them on the discussions of the "INF" treaty, which directly affected their defense planning. Just over a year later, Ukraine is at the center of American politics.

Russia plays a chord with European concerns, thanks to Trump

A few months after Bolton returned to Washington, preparations began to withdraw from the INF Treaty. But the withdrawal from the treaty required consulting with the allies of the United States in the European Union, especially in NATO, who saw that abolishing the treaty would be in Russia's interest and increase its threat to them, despite their conviction that Russia had repeatedly violated the treaty.

When Bolton landed in Moscow, US Ambassador John Huntsman met him and told him that the Russians were playing on European fears and America abandoning them, leaving them defenseless.

The author adds that President Trump, unfortunately, announced the intention of the United States to withdraw from the Treaty early, which confused the accounts of the US State Department. In late October, when Bolton landed in Moscow, US Ambassador John Huntsman met him and told him that the Russians were playing on European fears and America abandoning them, leaving them defenseless.

Upon meeting Bolton with Patrushev, he told him that Russia was violating the treaty and not abiding by its provisions, and after the increased capabilities of China, Iran and other countries, it became impossible to universalize the treaty.

The situation of China and technological changes make the treaty unrealistic

The writer says we tried to grasp the effects of Trump's hasty statements, but he returned again in a press interview to his usual statements without consulting with those around him, saying: "I am ending the agreement. Russia violated it and I finish it. " Asked if this constituted a threat to Putin, Trump replied: "It is a threat to whomever you want. This includes China, and other countries, they cannot play the non-compliance game on us. "

The author states that the next day, he met with Russian Defense Minister Sergei Shoigu, who seemed less interested in the INF Treaty. He said that Trump's message was clear and tolerating no ambiguity, and that the Russians had clearly received it. He added, "Under the current circumstances, the treaty has become unrealistic; Because of China and the technological changes that have occurred since the treaty was signed in 1987 ».

Shoigu preferred to try to rewrite the treaty to attract others to join it. "Our unilateral withdrawal was only favorable to our common enemies, and the reference was clear to China." Bolton recalls that he met with Russian President Putin, who made it clear to the media that he was not satisfied with the US withdrawal from the INF Treaty.

The Russians do not need the Iranian presence in Syria

Bolton discussed what happened in his meeting with Putin regarding Syria, as he indicated that after withdrawing from the Iranian nuclear deal, the United States wants to re-impose sanctions on Iran, and Putin acknowledged America's view that the Iranian people are tired of the regime, but he warned that the declaration A war against them economically would boost the regime's support. At the end of the meeting, the Americans joked about their position on the killing of Saudi journalist Jamal Khashoggi, and he said that Russia would sell weapons to the Saudis if America did not, which is undoubtedly true, and explains Trump's desire not to undo the military deals concluded at that time, according to Bolton.

Bolton concluded the chapter by noting that the United States announced its formal withdrawal from the treaty on February 1, 2019, and the Russians immediately announced their suspension of any new negotiations related to arms control.

7. Trump is looking for a way out from Syria and Afghanistan, but he does not find it

The seventh chapter of Bolton's book notes that the war against "extremist Islam" began long before September 11 and will continue after it as well, which is a reality that Trump did not like and treated as unreal, and he fought an endless war in the Middle East without setting a plan. Knit withdrawal.

Syria: Lawrence of Arabia ... calling your office

After the American response to Assad's use of chemical weapons, Syria re-emerged on the scene, against the backdrop of Turkey's arrest of the priest Andrew Burson on charges of conspiring with Fethullah Gulen.

Erdogan - whom Bolton called "Lawrence of Arabia" in this chapter of his book - spoke with Trump by phone about the Bronson case, and also raised the issue of the conviction of the Turkish Halkbank official, Muhammad Atila, accused of violating the sanctions imposed on Iran.

The author notes that this file carried a direct threat to Erdogan and his family. To accuse them of using the bank for personal purposes, especially after his son-in-law became Minister of Finance.

Finally, Erdogan questioned the legislation

presented in Congress that would halt the purchase of the F-35 because Ankara was intending to purchase the Russian S440 air defense system. If this legislation is passed, this deal could lead to sanctions on Turkey for breaching the sanctions imposed on Russia.

Closing the embassy or increasing sanctions? ... Trump's options for punishing Turkey

Bolton says: Although the media portrayed Trump as anti-Muslim, it did not understand - even as leaders in Europe and the Middle East tried to explain this - that Erdogan himself is a radical Islamist, busy transforming Turkey from the secular state of Ataturk to Islamic Turkey, and supports the Muslim Brotherhood and groups Another extremist in the Middle East, and he funds Hamas and Hezbollah.

The author notes that the US President was tired of procrastinating over Bronson's release, so he decided to punish Turkey by increasing tariffs on steel by 50% and on aluminum by

20%.

Turkey suggested releasing Bronson in exchange for dropping the investigations into Halkbank, and after consulting with Pompeo and Mnuchin, the US administration found that the matter was pending in the hands of the South New York Court. Because the value of sanctions breaching is worth $ 20 billion.

Trump's position has fluctuated at this point. Between thinking about closing the embassy in Ankara and expelling the Turkish ambassador, to increasing sanctions. Then the Turkish position changed after the deterioration of the economy, and this was evident in the hearing held on October 12th. Bronson was released after being convicted of espionage and other charges, as the writer saw it as a fulfillment of Erdogan's domestic political interests.

Bolton recounts later, in the same chapter, that Erdogan handed Trump, during the G20 summit in Buenos Aires, a court memorandum presented by the Halkbank defense, and Trump quickly examined it, then he said that he was confident that this issue had nothing to do with the sanctions on Iran. He added, "The people working in the New York court are Obama's followers, if they were my followers, they would solve the matter early."

Trump's desire to get out of Iraq weakened his position vis-à-vis Iran

Meanwhile in Syria, the situation was tense, and Bolton discussed the issue of military intervention there with officials. In Iraq, on September 8, Shiite militias attacked the US embassy in Baghdad and its consulate in Basra, and Iran launched missiles against US targets in Erbil.

And when Kelly brought the matter to Trump, he simply replied that he wanted to get out of there, and thus the American response was limited to condemning Iran's role in the attack, and here Bolton asks frowningly: What lesson did he teach Iran and its militias from our complete absence?

The repercussions of the American withdrawal from Syria through the eyes of the National Security Adviser

Then the world's attention turned to the issue of Turkey's invasion of northern Syria, which Erdogan was aiming at curbing the Kurds, while America believed that it was its duty to protect them because they stood by it in the fight against ISIS, which would cast a shadow over any alliance with other parties later.

"The United States is ready to withdraw from Syria, if Turkey pledges to continue fighting ISIS."

Trump to Erdogan

On September 14, Trump and Erdogan spoke by phone, and the US President said: The United

States is ready to withdraw from Syria, if Turkey pledges to continue fighting ISIS, and Erdogan promised to do so.

Trump entrusted the pullout to Bolton, who was wondering if that was part of his campaign promises. The National Security Adviser considered that the withdrawal would have disastrous consequences; On the one hand, it will lead to an increase in the power of ISIS, and on the other side, it will undoubtedly increase Iran's influence.

"A crushing defeat for America's policy and its credibility in the world"

The allies objected to the withdrawal, and Macron begged Trump not to do so. What Erdogan is interested in is getting rid of the Kurds only, and thus he may accept a settlement with ISIS.

After the media tension that coincided with

Bolton's visit to Israel before Ankara to complete the withdrawal agreement, and what he declared and raised Turkey's concern, it became clear that leaving Syria conflicts with the protection of the Kurds. Trump's opinion at the time was that Turkey had been preparing for a long time to attack the Kurds, and he wanted this to happen and our soldiers are not there, and that this is a civil war that America does not want to intervene in.

The scene in northern Syria until the time of Bolton's resignation was the fall of the ISIS caliphate, but with the persistence of the danger, the deterioration of negotiations over the formation of international forces, and Turkey's drowning in its economic and domestic problems.

When Trump issued his decision to withdraw in October 2019, Bolton had left the White House, a decision which Bolton describes as a crushing defeat for US policy and its credibility around the world.

Reasons why Trump and Bolton object to US forces remaining in Afghanistan

Trump believed - and he was right, as Bolton sees it - that he gave Mattis all the powers to eliminate the Taliban and ISIS. While the goal was achieved in Iraq and Syria, the opposite happened in Afghanistan. And this is all because of Trump, who believed he was right in 2016, even after the failure of the US military in 2017 and 2018.

Trump objected to the presence of US forces in Afghanistan for two reasons: The first is; That he pledged in his election campaign to end the endless war, and the second; The continuing faltering economy and security made him rush to put an end to federal spending.

Bolton's primary objection to ending the war was that the United States was not the one who started it in the first place, and therefore it cannot end once Washington wants it.

Bolton stressed that the purpose of these wars is not to build more beautiful and safer countries, but to protect America from a new 9/11, he said.

Trump to Mattis: Let Russia take care of ISIS in Afghanistan

Bolton met Trump who said the situation is bad there; We were defeated, and they know that. Mattis added: ISIS is still in Afghanistan. Trump responded: Let Russia take care of them, for we are thousands of kilometers away and we are still in the crosshairs of their targets, due to a stupid decision by a person named George Bush. We drowned in this swamp and millions of people were killed, and trillions were spent and we are not over. distance.

Pompeo asked for a period of 90 days before making the decision to withdraw, so Trump refused, reasoning that the longer the period becomes his war, and he does not like to lose a war. Mattis replied that it has become your war since I took office! He said: Therefore, I should have finished it immediately.

Bolton: Either we will fight terrorism on its soil or it will chase us to our own home

In his book, Bolton evokes the facts of this debate, and was of the opinion that the United States should fight terrorism on his land, and Dunford agreed that America would be attacked in its own house if it withdrew its forces from there.

The author continues in his book: I thought that we had to answer three questions before making a decision to withdraw, namely: Will the Afghan government collapse after our exit? And when? And at what speed will the terrorist groups move after our withdrawal? How much time do they need to organize an attack on the United States? The withdrawal order was pending until I left the White House.

8. Chaos is a way of life ... When does Trump officially start his day?

In chapter eight of his book, Bolton reviews aspects of Trump's life inside the White House, and how his official day begins close to lunchtime, because he does not do any activity in the morning, but rather makes phone calls from his residence with various spectra, and sometimes with government officials.

This pattern followed by Trump, the author compares it to the ordinary day of President George HW Bush: White House chief of staff during his term, John Sanuno, said he would start his official day at 8 am.

Trump's revenge tendencies and his reluctance to attend funerals

Bolton also spoke about Trump's revenge tendencies towards certain people, including John McCain, and then his decision to withdraw the security clearance of former CIA director

John Brennan, after Trump accused him of spying on his campaign in 2016, which was exacerbated by repeated Brennan appeared in the media and criticized Trump after taking office.

Some officials tried to dissuade Trump from withdrawing security clearances, reminding him that no president had ever made such decisions. Trump yielded to them, but quickly repeated his act, even more harshly.

Trump sparked another controversy about not attending funerals, which began with the funeral of Barbara Bush in 2018, and then the funeral of McCain last August, as Bolton mentions in his book.

"They will not give me their votes again if I do not close the borders."

The issue of illegal immigration was the main initiative put forward by Trump; He insisted on closing the border with Mexico to immigrants, had it not been difficult to implement this, given the United States' asylum policy.

Trump's view in this regard was that "the borders must be closed. The people elected me to do this, and now they will not elect me again if I do not fulfill my promise."

A "stark contrast" ... this is how Trump dealt with the Khashoggi case

The author states that in the midst of the immigration debate, the murder of Saudi journalist Jamal Khashoggi was raised at the Saudi embassy in Istanbul. He added that Trump's handling of the issue was in stark contrast to his usual approach to decision-making.

The Saudis published their story about the events related to the killing of Khashoggi, and of course that story did not receive the acceptance of analysts, who discovered that it would not change, especially after Trump approved it, and announced not to stop arms sales to Saudi Arabia, and declared his support for the Saudi monarch, Prince Muhammad bin Salman, and confirmed "Whether he did it (killing Khashoggi) or not, we will stand by Saudi Arabia."

The search for a replacement for Trump's ambassador to the United Nations

This chapter also examines the crises that arose due to the inefficiency of President Trump's ambassador to the United Nations, Nikki Haley, in managing the affairs of the sanctions imposed on Russia in the wake of the US attack on Syria.

Matters were compounded by the US withdrawal from the Human Rights Council, something Trump agreed to, and recommended by his advisers at an Oval Office meeting with Pompeo and Haley.

Trump asked Haley, "How is it going?" She answered, speaking about trade negotiations with China, which was not at the core of its responsibilities. As a result, Haley resigned in 2020, and the replacement of departing administration officials became difficult, especially with the approaching end of Trump's term.

Trump's condition was to choose a female to replace Halle, as Bolton explains in his book. And decided to choose the ambassador of the United States to Canada, Kelly Craft, to assume this position.

9. Venezuela .. Why does America consider the Maduro regime a threat?

The ninth chapter of Bolton's book touched on Venezuela, stating that its illegal regime presented an opportunity for the Trump administration, but it did not make good use of it. It was not fully confident of the success of supporting the efforts of the Venezuelan opposition to oust Nicolas Maduro, the heir to Hugo Chavez.

Maduro's authoritarian regime was a threat due to its association with Cuba, and its openness to Russia, China and Iran, as described by the author. Moscow's undeniable danger was also military and financial. It spent significant resources to support Maduro, and took control of the oil and gas industry in Venezuela, which caused losses to the United States.

The big bang took place in Venezuela on Friday (January 11), after the new young president of the National Assembly, Juan Guaidó, declared at a huge rally that Maduro's fraudulent re-election in 2018 was illegal. The assembly declared the presidency vacant.

Under Chavez, and now Maduro, Venezuela's revenue from oil-related exports has fallen from roughly 3.3 million barrels of oil per day, when Chávez took power in 1999, to nearly 1.1 million barrels per day in January 2019.

Historic phone call between Trump and Guaido

Bolton explained to Trump the political and economic steps that should be taken against Maduro, but Trump was skeptical that Maduro would fall, saying he was "very smart and very strong."

Tensions were running high inside Venezuela. Bolton and Pence spoke to Juan Guaido, and he responded positively. He said Venezuela is very happy with the support the United States is providing.

The Security Council met on Saturday, January 26th. Pompeo attacked the Maduro regime, and European members said that Maduro either had eight days to call the elections or they would recognize Guaido, and that was a major improvement in the position of the European Union, according to the book.

On January 30, Bolton's office was filled with many people to hear Trump's call with Guaido at around 9 am. Trump said the call was historic. Guaido thanked Trump for his calls for democracy and his strong leadership, which made Bolton smiling. Trump said it was an honor for me to speak with him, and the call ended.

The splits that Washington sought began to appear in Venezuela

On February 13, Colombian President Ivan Duque visited Trump at the White House, and the debate focused on Venezuela. Trump asked the Colombians if he should talk to Maduro six months ago, and Duque said, unequivocally, that it would be a huge victory for Maduro, which means it would be a bigger mistake to talk to him now. Trump agreed, which greatly delighted Bolton.

The author adds in his book: "On the other hand, the opposition negotiations with the main regime figures made clear the validity of their view that the cleavages we sought were beginning to emerge. Overcoming years of mistrust was not easy, but we tried to show that the opposition and Washington are serious about amnesty and avoid criminal prosecutions for past transgressions.

How much influence does Cuba have in Venezuela?

Bolton asked how much influence Cuba would have in Venezuela. He decided that the New York Times understood the problem; A main story was published on March 17th that narrated how Cuban "medical aid" was used to support Maduro among Venezuela's poor, and those who did not wish to follow Maduro's orders were denied support.

The article also showed the extent of Cuba's penetration of the Maduro regime and the poor conditions in Venezuela. In addition, a senior Venezuelan general who defected to Colombia described the extent of corruption within the country's health system, adding more evidence of corruption within the system.

The Wall Street Journal also published an article shortly thereafter detailing Maduro's loss of support among Venezuela's poor, something we had believed since the start of the insurgency in January.

Trump's note: "Do not wear a wedding ring and look younger than her real age."

Bolton noted that on March 27, Guaido's wife, Fabiana Rosales, arrived at the White House to meet Pence in the Roosevelt room, and then Trump greeted Fabiana Rosales and the others warmly.

Everyone heard Fabiana describing how bad things are in Venezuela. And the completely unexpected outcome of the meeting was what Trump concluded, that Fabiana does not wear a wedding ring, and looks younger than her real age.

The main obstacle to "liberating Venezuela": the Cuban presence and Russian support

Bolton explained that over the ensuing few months, the Venezuelan economy deteriorated, and the president of the International Committee of the Red Cross told him, after his visit to Venezuela, that he had not seen hospitals in such a condition since his last trip to North Korea.

Negotiations have resumed between the opposition and key regime figures. The opposition struggled to find a new strategy after the April 30th failed.

The author believes that what is now standing in the way of a major obstacle to "the liberation of Venezuela" is: the Cuban presence, supported by Russian financial resources.

If Cuba's military and intelligence networks leave the country; The Maduro regime will be in a dangerous and possibly shattered state, and everyone understands this fact, especially Maduro.

The inexperienced opposition has made some tactical mistakes, yet Bolton insists that the United States should not back down. He says: All the credit to those who risked their lives in Venezuela to free their citizens, and shame on those they thought badly, and Venezuela would be free.

10. The thunder coming from China

Bolton predicts at the beginning of Chapter 10 of his book that "the economic and geopolitical relationship between America and China will shape international relations in the twenty-first century," noting that Deng Xiaobin's decision to convert the Chinese economy from traditional communism in 1978, and America's decision to recognize the People's Republic of

China in 1979. They were a turning point in the relationship between the two countries.

The Chinese Dragon: The Economy at the Service of Political and Military Interests

According to Bolton, it was hoped that China would take steps toward openness and economic cooperation, and achieve a good level of democracy, but what it did was the complete opposite. After joining the World Trade Organization, it stole intellectual property for some technological products, discriminated against foreign investors, and got involved. In corrupt practices, the "debt trap" diplomacy followed the cover of projects such as the "One Belt - One Road" initiative, and it continued to dominate the economy.

China also sought to achieve political and military benefits from the economy, through companies that are in fact tools of the Chinese army and intelligence, and by engaging in violent cyber warfare that targeted private foreign interests, but also government secrets, according to the book.

On the other hand, the capacity of the Chinese army was growing. It has become in possession of the most powerful cyber warfare program, built a "blue water navy" (to operate internationally through the deep waters of the open ocean) for the first time in five hundred years, and has increased its arsenal of nuclear weapons, ballistic warheads, etc., a shift that the author considers a threat to America's strategic interests and those of its friends. And its allies around the world.

Trump is wooing China and mixes between personal and presidential

The book touched on the Chinese telecom company "ZTE", which committed major violations regarding the sanctions imposed on Iran and North Korea. The court succeeded in convicting it, and then allowed it to work under criminal supervision that revealed massive violations and subsequently banned it in the American markets.

Then, after a phone call with the Chinese president pledging to lift the sanctions on the company, Trump published a tweet confirming that the company was back in business. Because millions of jobs have been lost in China due to sanctions. And here Bolton asks: How long have we started worrying about jobs in China? To add: Trump could not distinguish between his personal interest and the presidential affair.

During the meeting that brought together the two presidents in Buenos Aires, Trump asked Jinping to increase purchases of US agricultural crops (to gain the agricultural states' votes), and promised to reduce tariffs in return.

Bolton asserts that Trump did not want to condemn China for any violations, regardless of the size of the Huawei case, the Hong Kong demonstrations, or the violence against Aliens. So as not to impede the course of trade negotiations between the two countries.

Corona pandemic ... the last typhoon from China

Bolton believes that this pandemic will remain under study for years to come. "But the fingerprints of the Chinese authoritarian regime are evident on it. There are suspicions about China's delay in disclosing information related to the virus, and even fabricating it; What impeded the efforts of the World Health Organization to obtain accurate information ».

As for Trump, given the presidential elections will be held this year, his management of the pandemic will be a factor in the election outcome. There are many criticisms that have already been directed at the Trump administration, whether in its management of the crisis, or the initial statements it made, which talked about containing the virus and the limited economic impact.

In this regard, Bolton draws two main conclusions:

The first: The need to do everything we can to make sure that China does not practice the "big lie" (inventing a lie and repeating it so that people believe it), and to tell the whole truth about China's behavior, "something that Trump hesitated to do", otherwise we will all face many consequences In the future.

The second: After we have seen the disastrous impact of this virus, we have to deal with biological and chemical weapons with the same caution that we deal with nuclear weapons. In fact, the combination of the Biosecurity Department and the Department in Charge of Weapons would increase the vigilance towards biological threats to the American people.

11. Trump is heading to North Korea again

More than six months have passed since the Singapore summit and there has been no progress worth noting, and after the 2018 congressional elections ended, arranging another summit between Trump and Kim was inevitable, something Bolton expressed his frustration with at the start of the eleventh chapter of his book.

The author spoke sarcastically about his meeting with Kim Jong Cheol, Kim Jong Un's older brother, in the Oval Office for 90 minutes, and indicated that it was worse than the surgery he had previously scheduled for that period, but it was necessary to prepare for the Hanoi summit, which was Glad it passed without a disaster or concessions.

Trump's policy with Kim: 'Ditch the girl before she ditches you'

Trump had expected three possible outcomes from this summit: a big deal, a small deal, or "I will leave." But he immediately rejected the "small deal"; Because it would mean weakening the sanctions, and ruling out the "big deal";

Because Kim is not ready to make a strategic decision to abandon nuclear weapons. As for the idea of "I will leave", it was repeated repeatedly, which means that Trump was prepared for this scenario, or perhaps he preferred it, based on his conviction that it was necessary to "abandon the girl before she abandoned you."

At the time, Kim offered that North Korea give up its nuclear facilities at Yongbyon, in exchange for the removal of all UN Security Council sanctions imposed after 2016, Pompeo said. But Bolton saw it as a ruse; Pyongyang is giving it much-needed lifespan while giving the Americans little, given the many other nuclear facilities North Korea has.

Bolton mentions that all Trump cares about is: the political implications, and indicates that his attention has always been focused on the ballot box.

Kim strikes a chord with Trump's feelings

Trump kept his word and raised the issue of Japanese kidnappers with Kim. But regarding the essence of the talks, Bolton points out once again that the president may be moving in the right direction, and then for the slightest reason his positions will turn 180 degrees completely opposite. He describes how, in his meeting with the North Korean leader, he was interested in Fox News covering the testimony of his former lawyer, Michael Cohen, before Congress.

Kim was so angry and frustrated that Trump had not given him what he wanted, while the US President was exhausted, angry, and frustrated at not reaching a satisfactory deal. Once again, Bolton states that all Trump cares about is: the political implications, and points out that his attention has always been focused on the ballot box.

Kim affirmed that he does not want anything that could harm his American counterpart politically, but Bolton concedes, saying: "Kim was cleverly playing on Trump's feelings, and I was worried that he would succeed."

Why do we impose sanctions on a country 7,000 miles away from us?

Trump asked Bolton: With what logic we can "impose sanctions on the economy of a country 7,000 miles away," to which he replied, "Because they are building nuclear weapons and missiles that can kill Americans." The president agreed, saying, "It's a good point." Then he went to Pompeo, and Trump told him about what he had with Bolton, and he replied in the affirmative: "Of course, sir."

But after that round ended, Bolton concluded that Trump was following the same failed approach that the previous three administrations followed, and he was doomed to reach the same failed result, citing some of the president's surprising tweets that were causing them frustration, and his constant conviction - even in this context - That Washington's allies have not paid enough. The American president not only wanted to share the burden, but also to gain a profit from these discussions.

Trump and Kim Jong Un meet in Hanoi, the capital of Vietnam.

The future of dealing with the North Korean file

The author expects North Korea to remain the focus of the White House during the 2020 election campaign, but what cannot be predicted is Kim's position; Will he take advantage of the conditions that the United States is going through in an election year and lure Trump into making a "bad deal"? To repeat the mistakes of his predecessor? Or will he rule out the possibility of striking a deal with Trump, and thus choose to wait until a more flexible Democratic president with less foreign policy experience ascends?

Whatever the answer, Bolton confirms at the conclusion of this chapter that North Korea will not stop seeking to possess full nuclear capabilities, a critical situation that Washington could have avoided, only if it decided to act decisively early, expressing his hope that the opportunity will be given to stop the disaster before it occurs.

12. This is how Trump lost his way, then fear seized him

The more the United States' attention diverts from Iran, and the more it falls on the Trump map in particular; Bolton knew that Tehran's same behavior would help them bring it back to the top of the president's agenda, and the Islamic Republic did not disappoint him, as he points out at the beginning of Chapter Twelve of his book.

This was not only due to Iran's nuclear weapons, nor its ballistic missile programs, but to its continuing role as the "global central bank of terror" and its aggressive military presence throughout the Middle East, as Bolton described it.

Classification of the Revolutionary Guard as a terrorist organization ... supporters and fearful

Bolton was in favor of designating the Revolutionary Guard a terrorist organization, and Trump and Pompeo agreed, but the US Treasury Secretary, Stephen Mnuchin, feared the wide-ranging consequences that would ensue, and the government bureaucracy helped him block the move. It was that the US administration ultimately ended up applying a policy of "maximum pressure" on Iran.

Bolton was disagreeing with Mnuchin in assessing economic concerns, and despite his acknowledgment of the theoretical danger to the dollar in the world, he believed that this risk did exist, regardless of the effects of US sanctions.

Mnuchin feared that the excessive use of the

sanctions weapon would nullify the magic of this tool, or raise oil prices globally in the event of tightening oil sanctions against Iran (or Venezuela), or even undermine the dominance of the dollar over the international monetary system, and encourage others, such as Russia and China, to Concluding their financial dealings in euros, cross-trade (bartering products or services for the same without the need to pay money), and other methods of bypassing US sanctions.

But Bolton was disagreeing with Mnuchin in assessing economic concerns, and despite his acknowledgment of the theoretical danger to the dollar in the world, he believed that this danger did exist, regardless of the effects of US sanctions. He also disagreed with the Treasury Secretary in assessing military concerns, inferring that he effectively proposed the sanctions that the Bush administration applied to Saddam Hussein's regime, even if he admitted that that alone was not sufficient.

"If only the American economic swords were

sharper."

Bolton was not alone in adopting this opinion, but the US Secretary of Commerce, Wilbur Ross, also believed that, as he said - in the context of Venezuela - that "Mnuchin was often concerned with protecting American companies that slept with the enemy more than he was concerned with getting the job done. Which we were trying to accomplish ».

The author of the book comments: "If the American economic swords were sharper in the Trump era; We would have accomplished much more than that.

But Mnuchin's arguments found an ear in the White House, especially since Trump had always believed that Washington's allies had not done enough in this regard, a view supported by Bolton, especially with regard to the Iranian file. France, Germany, and the United Kingdom have been bailing out the nuclear deal, instead of pressuring Iran's mullahs.

Netanyahu, Bin Salman and Bolton were trying to topple the Iranian regime

In parallel, Israeli Prime Minister Benjamin Netanyahu, Saudi Crown Prince Mohammed bin Salman, and Bolton were trying to overthrow the Iranian regime, while Tehran was preparing to launch a major campaign against US interests in the Middle East, targeting the US embassy in Baghdad, and had already launched attacks targeting tankers and facilities Gulf oil.

After criticizing the State Department's approach to making concessions, Bolton advises the next US administration to reform Mnuchin's approach immediately, so that everyone realizes that economic sanctions are an effective weapon, not a tool Washington feels guilty about whenever it resorted to.

On the map of US national security priorities ...

Where is the Iranian threat?

The US National Security Strategy used to list China, Russia, North Korea, and Iran in order under the classification: Main Threats. This means, in the opinion of Defense Secretary James Mattis, that Iran was a "level four" threat, and thus it did not implicitly deserve this much of interest.

Although this strategy was formulated before Bolton joined the administration, its content has always been explained by the fact that these four countries, taken together rather than in order, represent the "first level" of threat. Within this "first level", Iran may be in fourth place, but only because the strategists do not believe that it possesses nuclear weapons.

Trump's sudden leaps from diplomatic pact to all-out war

Bolton therefore argued that if US policy is to

prevent Iran from obtaining nuclear weapons, the United States should be prepared to use military force if necessary.

And the author adds: A large number of Trump's people wanted to go to war sooner, but that never happened because of the president who was jumping within seconds from the idea of reaching an agreement, to the adoption of total war.

For 25 years, he cautioned, people were unwilling to do what was necessary to stop North Korea from becoming a nuclear-weapon state, which led us to confront North Korea, which already has nuclear weapons now, and to avoid a repeat of this outcome with Iran, we had to We are intensifying the pressure economically, politically and militarily.

Trump's condition for striking Iran: That the Arabs pay the bill

But Trump did not agree to give an absolute mandate to the military options, and stipulated that the Arab allies pay the bill for any operations carried out by his country, indicating that the United States should have acquired Iraqi oil after its invasion in 2003, and it should also obtain Venezuela's oil after the overthrow of President Nicolas Maduro.

"I don't care if ISIS returns to Iraq."

Trump

When it came to the remaining US forces in Iraq, Trump asked: "Why don't we get them out? Didn't we get rid of ISIS in Syria? " "What I heard next was shocking," Bolton says, "but I clearly remember hearing him say, 'I don't care if ISIS returns to Iraq.'"

Gulf concern about American weakness towards Iran

The Emiratis were very concerned about America's failure to respond to Iranian provocations, the increased flow of missiles and drones to the Houthis and Shiite militias in Iraq, and Iran's assistance to the Taliban and ISIS in Afghanistan.

Despite Bolton's reassurances, the crown prince of Abu Dhabi and the princes of the Gulf were convinced of Trump's weakness, while the Iranians were convinced that he was not serious. "While Tehran was pursuing its pursuit of nuclear weapons, we were sitting and watching the grass grow (in the presence of boredom)," Bolton says, commenting on the atmosphere.

Why did Bolton consider resigning so many times?

When Trump asked Bolton once for his opinion on a statement he was considering writing on Twitter, just before a scheduled phone call with Mohammed bin Salman, the National Security Adviser did not object, and he said to himself:

"Why object? Things have gone completely wrong before, so how can some tweets make it worse?"

And with Trump's reluctance to take a decisive stance, and his desire to go militarily further than his advisors suggest, Bolton says that he thought about resigning several times, saying to himself: If this is the way we will make decisions in times of crisis, then what is the desired benefit of my survival?

13. From counterterrorism in Afghanistan to the canceled Camp David negotiations

John Bolton opens Chapter Thirteen by listing the goals that he - along with Trump's most senior advisers - would like to achieve in Afghanistan:

The first is to prevent the return of ISIS and Al Qaeda, and stop their terrorist attacks against America.

And second: monitoring nuclear weapons programs in Iran in the west and Pakistan in the east.

However, he continues, "The hardest part was getting Trump to agree, and then stick to his decision."

Briefing session explaining the Pentagon's mission in Afghanistan

A briefing for the presentation of the information was scheduled for March 15th, with the attendance of then Acting Secretary of Defense Patrick Shanahan and Joint Chiefs of Staff Chairman Joseph Dunford.

Bolton spoke to Trump to explain to him that the session would include the Pentagon's explanation of the military mission in Afghanistan; Based on his instructions to reduce the American presence, the President asked him: "Would that not harm the negotiations?"

Bolton replied in the negative.

During the session, Trump asked, "How are the negotiations going?" Dunford replied: "Our current strategy is to reduce violence; What this means is that we can accomplish our continuing mission of combating terrorism and other tasks in practice with fewer resources."

"Let's conclude a great and wonderful agreement. If they do a bad thing (meaning if the Taliban violate the agreement), we will blow up their damned country into a million pieces."

Trump

The US State Department's negotiating objectives in Afghanistan

In his book, Bolton says, "What worried me most was that the State Department's negotiating goals were completely separate from what I had previously defined regarding our goals for the negotiations." So, Bolton called Trump and told him it was up to him to decide whether to allow the US envoy to Afghanistan, Khalilzad, and the State Department, to act with complete independence in negotiations, but the National Security Adviser feared that what Trump wanted was dangerous.

Trump referred to Khalilzad, saying, "I don't even know who he is, do what you think is best." Then that same morning Bolton met Khalilzadeh, who told him that Pompeo had ordered him not to communicate with him (Bolton); Because he was undermining Pompeo's image with Trump. This prompted Bolton to question whether Pompeo's real motive was to get credit in Afghanistan.

Journalists are seen by Trump ... "trash should be executed"

In one of the meetings, Trump asked several questions about the deal, especially the clause of the prisoner and hostage exchange between the Taliban and the Afghan government (the clause that was in the interest of the Taliban more, according to the author), and this is what Trump did not like at all.

During the discussion, Trump stressed, "I prefer not to make an agreement than to conclude a bad agreement, as it is worse than just withdrawing from negotiations." However, he quickly switched his speech to complaining about the leaks after CNN's coverage of this meeting earlier.

The President said: "These people should be executed; They are just scum." He added, " The Ministry of Justice must arrest these journalists and force them to reveal their sources, and then the leaks will stop. "

There is no well-thought-out military strategy in the Trump administration

Trump had apparently decided to approve the Pompeo-Khalilzadeh deal. Bolton referred to what Trump said: "Let's make a great, wonderful agreement. If they do something bad (meaning if the Taliban violate the agreement), we will blow their damned country into a million pieces."

In his book, Bolton comments on this position: This is simply a paradigm analysis of Trump's behavior, and falls short of a well-thought-out military strategy.

Thus Trump called off negotiations with the Taliban at Camp David

On the evening of September 7, after a suicide bombing in Afghanistan, Trump could not restrain it; He tweeted announcing the cancellation of negotiations with the Taliban and the Afghan president, about which a secret meeting was scheduled to take place at Camp David, saying: "It is not known to everyone that the Taliban leaders and the Afghan president would have met me secretly, each one alone at Camp David on Sunday. They were on their way to the United States this evening, but I canceled the meeting immediately after claiming responsibility for the attack in Kabul, which killed one of our brave soldiers and 11 others.

Trump added: "What kind of people are killing this number of people in order to strengthen their negotiating position? But they only made things worse. "If they are not able to accept a ceasefire during peace negotiations, then they probably do not have the means to negotiate a meaningful agreement."

The dangers of an agreement with the Taliban in Bolton's eyes

Trump resumed talks with the Taliban after Bolton resigned, and the agreement was signed on Saturday, February 29, 2020. "Signing this agreement with the Taliban represents an unacceptable danger to the citizens of America," Bolton wrote on Twitter that morning.

Former US National Security Adviser John Bolton concludes chapter thirteen of his book, saying: "The effects of the deal will not be apparent until after Trump leaves the White House, which Trump will bear in full, and he will be responsible for its consequences, whether political or military."

14. End of the poem

Bolton says at the start of Act Fourteen that throughout his tenure in the West Wing of the White House, Trump wanted to do what he wanted, based on what he knew and what he saw as his personal interest, and Ukraine was the best example of this.

The author notes that the incident of Russia's seizure of a number of Ukrainian ships in the Kerch Strait in the Crimea, prompted Trump to tell one of his favorite stories, which relate to his first call with German Chancellor Angela

Merkel, when I asked him: What will he do about Ukraine, so his response was that In turn, he asked her: What is she going to do about Ukraine?

At that time, the Americans asked the Russians to release the Ukrainian ships. So that Trump could hold a bilateral meeting with Putin in Buenos Aires on the sidelines of the G20 summit, but the Russians refused and said: The sailors will face criminal charges.

Trump: "Ukraine tried to overthrow me ... and I'm not interested in helping them"

Bolton reveals that Trump's lawyer, Rudy Giuliani, was the one who entered into his mind that the US ambassador in Kiev, Mary Jovanovich, was protecting Hillary Clinton, whose campaign was the subject of investigations in Ukraine, which prompted Trump to push Pompeo, the foreign minister, to fire her. .

Bolton says that Trump summoned him to his office, and there he found Giuliani who wanted to meet with Ukrainian President-elect Volodymyr Zelensky to discuss with him his country's investigations into Hillary Clinton's efforts to influence the 2016 campaign, or anything related to Hunter Biden and the 2020 elections.

Bolton believes that Trump believed that Ukraine was indeed responsible for Moscow's efforts to piracy the US election. This means that we should not help Ukraine even if it helps us stop further Russian advances there. "Ukraine tried to topple me ... and I'm not interested in helping them," Trump said.

In this chapter, Bolton also touches on the Trump call that led to his trial in Congress, and says that the call he listened to, and that Security Council employees transcribed, is not a "text" like that written by a court employee. When Bolton met with the National Security Council's legal advisor, John Eisenberg, to discuss how to record the calls, they decided to leave things as they are.

Trump is begging for help from outside to win the election

In 1992, when Bush Sr.'s aides asked him to ask foreign governments to help him in his faltering campaign against Bill Clinton, Bush and James Baker immediately refused, but Trump did just the opposite, the book says.

Bolton says they could have confronted Trump, refuting Giuliani's claims and arguing that it is not permissible to mortgage the interests of the US authorities for personal political gain. But he knows they would have failed in their endeavor, and it may have left more vacant sites in the White House.

Trump insisted that security aid to Ukraine not be released until they provide all Russian investigation materials related to Hillary

Clinton and Biden. Zelensky was not interested in being a party to American politics, though he was happy to investigate what happened in 2016, before he came to power.

At one point, the press began to smell the link between the withholding of military aid to Ukraine and Trump's preoccupation with the 2016 and 2020 elections, at which point Trump released the military aid to Ukraine around the time of the Russians' release of the Ukrainian sailors and ships.

The last conversation between Bolton and Trump before resigning

Bolton concludes the chapter with his resignation; On September 9, Trump summoned him to the Oval Office to complain about the press's coverage of Afghanistan and the cancellation of the Camp David meeting with the Taliban. "A lot of people don't like you," he told him. They say you leaked information, and not a member of the team. "

Bolton responded that he had been the target of a campaign of negative leaks in recent months, and invited him to read the positive stories about him in the "New York Times", "The Washington Post" and other newspapers explaining who was doing the leaks.

Then Trump pointed his finger to him, and said to him, "You have your plane," which prompted him to clarify that he travels on military planes on all his official trips, and this is the same policy that governs his predecessors.

Then Trump accused him of returning all National Security Council employees to their positions, including a large number of "deep state". Then Bolton got up and told him "If I want to leave, I will leave." Trump told him, "Let's talk about it in the morning."

Bolton says that was his last conversation with Trump, after which he submitted his letter of resignation to his assistant Christine Samolian, which he had written several months ago, to print it on a letter bearing the White House letterhead, and he began preparing to resign the next day.

The next day, he came to his office at regular business hours and asked Kristen to take the letter to Pence and several White House officials at 11:30. Trump tweeted around 11:50 to announce the news first, but Bolton was content to confront the tweet with the facts.

15. Focusing on Ukraine weakens Trump's impeachment effort

Bolton begins the fifteenth and final chapter of his book by noting that his resignation from the position of National Security Adviser on September 10, 2019 preceded the saga of Trump's impeachment, which he distanced himself from the details of, but at the same time confirms that Trump's behavior related to the accusations against him was extremely worrying. The interviewer accuses the media of being biased in their coverage according to private agendas.

Bolton asserts that "the president may not abuse the legitimate powers granted to the national government by making his personal interest synonymous with the national interest, or by fabricating excuses to conceal his pursuit of a personal interest under the guise of the national interest."

If the House of Representatives did not focus on the Ukrainian aspects of Trump's interests, whether political or economic, and instead focused on the broader pattern of Trump's behavior - including his lobbying campaigns on issues such as Halkbank, ZTE and Huawei - perhaps There was a greater chance of convincing others that he had committed "major crimes and misdemeanors," the author suggests.

Bolton points out that most of the important decisions that Trump made during his tenure were driven by re-election accounts, but partisanship dominated the entire impeachment battle, and the result was that those efforts failed to achieve their goal, and the real test facing Trump remains: the upcoming presidential election.

There are no secrets related to national security in these notes

Bolton's new book concludes at its end that many of Trump's national security decisions were based on politics, rather than on philosophy, strategy, foreign policy, or defensive justifications, and frustrated Trump's attempts to prevent his book from being published, which forced him to introduce Some adjustments, especially for quotations; So as not to fall under the misfortune of the ambushed president.

But Bolton confirms overall that he is committed - from the start - to what he pledged to preserve national security secrets, especially since he had a lot to say without having to reveal those secrets. He concludes his book by affirming that he still supports those views that he defended before, and put them here in his memoirs.

Made in the USA
Monee, IL
19 September 2022